Managing Your Moods:
A 30-Day Plan

From One Bipolar Survivor to Another

I0117220

Barbara Arner

chipmunkapublishing
the mental health publisher

Published by
Chipmunkapublishing
PO Box 6872
Brentwood
Essex CM13 1ZT
United Kingdom

http://www.chipmunkapublishing.com

Copyright © Barbara Arner 2012

Edited by Aleks Lech

ISBN 978-1-84991-806-0

Chipmunkapublishing gratefully acknowledge the support of Arts Council England.

Author Biography

Barbara Arner - (b. 12/31/76)

Barbara is 35 years of age and was diagnosed with bipolar disorder at the age of 19. She graduated from the University of Vermont in 2000 with a degree in studio art and psychology. She has pursued her art which consists of drawing, painting, photography, pottery, and sculpture. In the winter she works as a ski instructor in New Jersey. Barbara currently resides at the Jersey Shore where she enjoys writing, making art, and spending her days relaxing on the beach.

Contents

One day at a time.

I woke up this morning and wanted to die. I wanted to flat-out kill myself; end my life. I just wanted to end this depression; this living with bipolar disorder. But inside I knew that, more than that, I wanted to get better. And in a day, today, I did get better.

See, I've tried to kill myself before and thank God it just doesn't work. It saddens your family, it saddens yourself, and it is just not the answer. "A permanent solution to a temporary problem." Depression comes and goes. Moods swing up and down. You learn to live with them; you learn to cope with them. You learn to love and accept bipolar disorder; you learn to love and accept yourself.

Summer has always been a difficult time for me. Summer—most people are swimming, boating, and socializing, and I, on the other hand, want to stay home alone in my bed away from everything and everyone. I don't want to exercise, I don't want to eat healthy, and I don't want to take care of myself. But today I did and that made all the difference.

First, you have to care. You have to care to make the healthier decisions for yourself. You have to care about yourself. Even if you are suicidal, especially if you are suicidal, you have to care. You can get yourself better. You have to want to and only you can do it.

Having bipolar disorder is hard work. It is difficult and painful, but possible. Living with a mental illness—it's your friend, your enemy, your lifelong companion. Conquer it.

Day 1

Chart Your Moods

Charting your moods daily may seem tedious, boring, and unnecessary, but it helps. It helps to see the overall bigger picture of your mental illness—of your bipolar mood swings from depression to mania. Charting these moods daily may prevent a full-blown episode of severe depression or severe mania. If anything you can have insight into your mood patterns throughout the month. In addition to charting the severity of your mood, you can also track contributing factors such as your anxiety and irritability levels, your hours slept, your exercise, and your weight. Taking notes on events that may have impacted these mood swings may also be worthwhile.

By charting your illness it gives you information on your mood patterns. How often do you feel mildly depressed? When do you feel mildly manic? You have more insight into your illness. When I'm depressed, I see I've been sleeping too many hours. When I'm feeling good, I see I have been exercising. Tracking my weight also keeps it at bay.

By tracking your mood swings you get information on yourself and your illness. It is something you can share with your psychiatrist to give him a better idea on how you have been feeling throughout the month. Perhaps you'll need a medication adjustment if you've been feeling too depressed or too manic. You should not be suffering. You should be able to live and enjoy your life. Take responsibility for your illness and your life and start enjoying it. Try to chart your moods for the month. See what it reveals about you and your illness. It's a beginning.

Day 2

Relax

Re-lax: to release or bring relief from the effects of tension, anxiety, etc.

Relax. Bipolar disorder brings stress, tension, and pain. Relax. Do something pleasant; something you enjoy—or nothing at all. Relax.

I like to sit on the beach, feel the sun, and watch the waves to relax. It brings a sense of peace, calm, and tranquility. It soothes and comforts me. Relax. Do something to bring relief from the pain. Or do nothing.

Bipolar disorder may bring hurt, sadness, and frustration. It can be a living hell. Take time out from it and relax. Focus your mind elsewhere.

I have continually feared when I would get sick again. When would I become severely depressed again? Have a manic episode? Will I have to be hospitalized? Will my medication stop working? Will I lose control once again? Will I want to die? Relax. Relax the mind. Relax the body. Do something you enjoy. Do nothing.

Day 3

Exercise Daily

Everyone knows exercise works to help you feel better and stay healthy. But how many people make the effort to exercise? Do you? Why or why not? Can you? What do you like to do? What brings you pleasure? What is not dreadful? What will you choose to do?

Exercise works. I like to swim in the summer and ski in the winter. These are activities that I love to do. What do you love to do? Find something. Do something.

Swimming: the water touches my numb body and makes me feel good. Sometimes I take it nice and slow; sometimes I get all my energy out and swim fast. All that tension leaves my body and makes me feel good and relaxed.

Skiing: I love the challenge of steeper terrain and faster movements. Using my entire body. Exhausting myself. Having a good feeling going down the mountain. Pushing myself. Improving my skills. Taking on the challenge of skiing.

Exercise. Do something. Something you love.

Day 4

Banish Negative Relationships

Banish negative relationships. If someone makes you feel bad, hurts you, or makes you feel angry consider asking yourself, "It is worth sacrificing my health and my sanity to keep these people in my life? Is it worth my time and my energy?" If you are feeling worse and if your mental health is deteriorating reconsider these relationships.

I consider myself a very thoughtful, caring, and loving friend. My select friends I have love me. They express their love for me and are supportive in my life. How are your friends to you? Do they say nasty, hurtful, and unnecessary things? Do they make you feel bad? Reconsider them. It's worth your mental health and sanity. Think it through and banish negative relationships.

Day 5

Eat Healthy

Sometimes I do it and sometimes I don't. But, when I do eat healthy, it makes everything more manageable.

Eat healthy. Try to get rid of the junk food and eat fruit and vegetables, whole grains, and protein. It makes living with a mental illness better. You'll feel better.

Whenever I get depressed I never have the energy it takes to make a healthy meal. I don't shop for fruit and vegetables. I don't have the energy to cook. My body craves everything else and if I give in to sugar and fattening foods I feel worse. It's a difficult pattern to break, especially when you are depressed. Then eating poorly can lead to not exercising, further making it difficult to care for yourself: a vicious cycle. Try to eat healthy. It makes a difference.

Day 6

Take Your Meds

Medicine: a love/hate relationship. I've been taking psychiatric medicine for sixteen years. The truth be told—sometimes it works, sometimes it doesn't. Regardless, I still keep taking it.

I believe it decreases my symptoms and episodes. I hope it has. My manias have not been as severe as my first when I was not medicated. My depressions have improved by being on two antidepressants. It comes and goes. Bipolar in waves. I am off my medicine I took in my early years which caused weight gain and other side effects. I do believe in my medicine. I don't have any side effects now so some things have improved. But the truth is medicine does not cure you of bipolar disorder, but, hopefully, it lessens the severity and amount of episodes.

Having bipolar disorder can easily get one depressed, but having a good therapist who can walk you through these emotions helps. It comes in waves. Up and down. I believe medicine can help.

Day 7

See Your Therapist/Psychiatrist

I am fortunate: I have a good one. My psychiatrist also serves as my therapist. He guides me through my life. As he constantly says, "Do more of what you like and less of what you don't." He has made me happier, healthier, and a better person. He is dedicated, determined, and helps me accomplish my goals.

I've been seeing my psychiatrist regularly for about ten years. He has seen my development as a person and has been able to treat every symptom of my illness. Therapy is not always easy. It takes time, commitment, and a desire to stay well. It becomes a lifestyle. I hope if you have one he/she is a good one and you are benefiting from your treatment. A great one is even better. See your therapist.

Day 8

Stop

Bipolar disorder can get crazy. It can become unmanageable and unbearable. Sometimes you just have to physically stop. Take a moment to breathe and just stop.

Stop and think what you're doing, where you're going, and if you are happy. What can make you happier? Stop and listen to yourself. Bipolar disorder is difficult. Sometimes you are depressed, manic, psychotic, and anxious. Just stop. Give it some thought. Become at peace and at ease with your mental illness. Try to accept it. Live a better life because of it. Maybe you are more sensitive to others or perhaps you can empathize with others who have a mental illness. Maybe you have made great friends who have bipolar in which you can support each other. Bipolar disorder can make you a better person. It does not always have to be suffering, pain, and sadness. It can be tamed if you stop and just think a little.

Day 9

Be Thankful

I am thankful I have family, friends, and a psychiatrist who care. They care about me, my life, and how I am doing. They express their concerns—their thoughts. For these people I am thankful.

I am also thankful I have developed a peaceful, stress-free lifestyle. I work as an artist and ski instructor. I do not function well with stress. I get sick: manic, depressed, psychotic, and anxious. I have had to develop a lifestyle that works well for me. I've had to adjust myself to something that is possible, to something I can do, and enjoy. For this I am thankful.

I am also thankful I have become who I am today. I am more caring, considerate, and sensitive to others. I have more patience and understanding. I am a better person because of my illness. Be thankful.

Day 10

Calm the Voices

I can get that angry, raging voice: "Why me? Why do I have to manage an illness every day? I can't do this anymore. It's too difficult." It takes time and energy to change these thoughts. Take time to calm the voices.

Listen to music. Meditate. Pray. Do something that will calm you of the thoughts you are having. Especially the one of "I want to kill myself. I want to die." Listen to it and change it. Talk yourself out of these thoughts. When I have negative thoughts, I always try to look at the positive. What is good? What do I have? Who will miss me? I can't do that to them. After all, this is the only life I have. Change the negative voices. Talk yourself out of suicide. Stop raging. Become calm. Calm those harsh voices.

Day 11

Travel

Go away. Do something. See something new. It can be the next town over, another state, or another country. Travel. Enjoy yourself. Treat yourself to something new. Go alone or go with someone.

I used to not travel because of my illness. I was afraid I would get sick and have to be hospitalized. Now I just go, take my medicine, and call my psychiatrist if there's a problem. Yes, I hated to travel and for years I could not. I felt too sick; too awful.

I enjoy skiing now. I hope to travel more with skiing. This time I am not going to let my illness hold me back. Yes, I am going to be careful and cautious, but I am going to go. Travel.

Day 12

Stress Less

Stress is one of my ultimate triggers. If I experience stress, I get sick—usually manic and psychotic. It makes the bipolar experience much worse. It makes it painful.

Sometimes stress is inevitable. I have experienced school stress, work stress, and family stress—specifically my father dying. Life gets stressful, difficult, and unmanageable. What can you do to decrease your stress level? Make the adjustments.

Day 13

Play

Play requires taking the seriousness out of life; the seriousness of having to live with bipolar disorder by taking a fun break from it all.

What do you like to do to play? I like to play with my dog. She brings out happiness and joy in me. I love running with her, playing fetch on the beach, watching her swim, and seeing her have fun playing with other dogs. It brings a sense of enjoyment to me. I feel carefree and relaxed. She brings fun into my life and decreases the emotional pain. What can you do to ease your bipolar symptoms? Try to play and have some fun.

Day 14

Have a Reliable Confidante

This one is important. Sometimes it's a matter of life and death. You need support. Support from a friend, support from a family member—support from a loved one. You need someone. The right someone. If you have that person consider yourself fortunate.

When you have someone you can honestly confide in, it can make all the difference. If you are feeling desperate, feeling suicidal, talking to the right person can make the pain subside. If you have someone who listens, cares, and loves you it makes a difference. Choose your confidante well.

Day 15

Don't Kill Yourself

Does this even need to be explained? Do you understand that this is not the answer? Suicide—a permanent solution to a temporary problem. You can work through these emotions—believe you can, work through it, and it will pass. Don't kill yourself.

You hurt your family; you hurt your friends. Don't do it. I wish I could never say I've felt suicidal, but that is not the truth. Bipolar disorder can bring emotional pain. It can bring hurt, sadness, frustration, disappointment, and exhaustion. Sometimes you just cannot take it anymore. It is difficult to say the least. Sometimes you need a medication adjustment and sometimes talking to your confidante is enough. There are solutions to feeling suicidal.

Find what works best for you. Is it exercising? Is it relaxing? Taking a break? Do whatever you need to help the feeling pass. It will. It does. You can make it through. Don't kill yourself. It is not the answer. Give it some time. You will feel better again.

Day 16

Take a Break

Bipolar disorder is an intense experience. It is rarely filled with celebrations and fun. It can be filled with pain, loneliness, and sadness: hurt. And for a long time. Take a break.

What can you do to take a break? I love sitting on the beach. Sitting in the sun looking out into the water gives me a break from everything. I can relax. Sometimes even reading a book is too much. Sometimes just sitting is all I need and all I can do. Take a break. You are entitled to and deserve a break. You work hard at living with this illness. Take a break.

Day 17

Meditate

By taking the time to meditate you may gain a better perspective and understanding of yourself and your bipolar experience. Clearing out all the negative voices inside you may bring a sense of peace. A silence. Can you make the time to silence your bipolar experience? What can you do?

I like to make pottery. It is a very quiet, calming experience for me. I can relax and just be in the moment. Feeling soft clay going through my hands and being at peace. Sitting at the potter's wheel is a meditative process for me. I can just focus on making pottery and enjoying the silent experience. Bring some peace to your bipolar experience and meditate. Find a way that works for you.

Day 18

Love Someone

Being in love, expressing love, or feeling love brings natural chemicals through your brain. You feel the energy; the calm; the love. Love someone.

A person I loved with all my heart was my grandmother. I loved going to her house, sitting with her, and talking: our special moments. When the phone would ring when I was visiting, she would answer saying with love in her voice that I was visiting. We loved each other. I loved our moments together and sharing our lives. Love someone. It helps.

Day 19

Laugh

When you are depressed you rarely laugh. Laughter is foreign. If you have someone who makes you laugh when you are feeling down, it can make a difference.

My psychiatrist makes me laugh. I leave his office feeling better and a bit less depressed. Medication may not do it all for you. Sometimes you have to change your attitude—lighten up and laugh.

Day 20

Have Some Fun

When was the last time you had fun? Do you remember? What were you doing? If it has been a while try to have some fun. Choose to do something you enjoy and that brings you pleasure.

I love skiing. I have fun as a ski instructor and skiing with my co-workers. I laugh, it brings me pleasure, and it is something I like to do. The people and experience bring me joy.

Figure out what makes you have fun. And just do it.

Day 21

Sit

Sometimes you just have to sit and do nothing. It rests your mind; rests your worries. It brings a sense of peace and tranquility. It lets you stop thinking so much about everything. It lets you heal. And healing is what we all need. By sitting you take a step away from the bipolar experience and can gain a better perspective. Your mind can be at peace. You can take a moment for yourself and enjoy the nothingness. Just sit. It may help you. It helps me.

Day 22

Get Angry

Get angry. Assert yourself appropriately and express yourself. I believe that by turning your anger inward onto yourself you will become more depressed. We don't need to be more depressed.

Why are you angry? What is getting you angry? Is there something appropriate that can be done about the situation? Do it. Make your feelings and yourself better. Don't become more depressed, upset, or discontent. Do something about the anger you feel. Assert yourself, write out your feelings, make some art, express yourself. Express your anger. Let it pour out of you appropriately. Feel a sense of relief. Express your anger appropriately.

Day 23

Talk to a Friend

A friend is someone who supports you and loves you. Communicate with them. Talk. Have a conversation. One of support and one that gives hope.

I am very thankful I have my friends in my life. When you hear someone say that they care about you, it helps. If they remind you of the good person you are it eases the pain. Talk to a good friend.

Day 24

Distract Yourself

Get your mind off your problems. Do something else. I like to read. Distract yourself from the drama and the pain. Maybe see a movie. Do something to get your mind on something else for the moment. It may help.

Day 25

Change Your Meds

If it has been a while and they are not working, change them. Sometimes it takes trial and error to find an effective combination. Be patient. Wait it out. If you are feeling manic or depressed consider a medication adjustment or change. It could help.

I have been on so much medicine, some with unbearable side effects. I've stayed away from those. I don't experience any side effects with the medicine I'm on now. Take the time and be patient with finding the right combination that will work best.

Day 26

Change Your Therapist

Compatibility is important. You must like, trust, and respect your therapist. If you experience conflicts, if you feel uncomfortable, or you are not seeing improvement and advancement in your life, consider changing your therapist.

Day 27

Work Hard

Depression and mania are challenging, but the truth is that you have to work doing something. Anything. And whatever that may be it should be done well, and, hopefully, you can work hard, diligently, and productively. Something to keep you busy and to feel good; good about your life and good about yourself.

I've constantly struggled with maintaining a job. I think most jobs I've had have had to be terminated because of the intensity of my illness. Working is difficult while managing bipolar disorder, but something that works for you is possible.

Working as an artist and ski instructor come naturally to me. I've decided to make them both my professions. These choices evolved due not only to my interests, but to what works while managing my illness. I can make art any time I want and I can choose my own schedule as a ski instructor. I need the flexibility due to my bipolar episodes. Find something that works for you and work hard.

Day 28

Talk to Family

This can be a difficult one. How are you with your family? Can you talk to them? Can you talk about your illness with them? If so, then communicate. Tell them what you need and how they can help you. Family support is crucial.

My mother has endlessly given me emotional support. She listens, she cares, and she loves me. We communicate often. She has witnessed me experience my illness for the past sixteen years. She listens to every word I have to say and responds in the most caring, compassionate, and loving way. I am fortunate I have her for emotional support. Communicate with your family for more support.

Day 29

Have a Hobby

By having a hobby you can take your mind off yourself and enjoy something. You can take a much needed break.

I love to make art: drawing, painting, photography, pottery, or sculpting. It takes my mind off my problems and lets me create. I focus on my skills and push them to evolve. Making art can consume me. It brings a feeling of joy, satisfaction, and relief. Do something positive. Find a hobby you enjoy.

Day 30

Go Outside

Staying inside, remaining depressed, only makes the illness worse. Go outside. Even if it is just to sit. Try going outside. Maybe you'll end up doing more: going for a walk, playing with your dog, playing with your child. Being outside may make a difference. Being in the sunshine, feeling the sun, may make you feel better. I know it does—it helps me. It may help your mood, too. Go outside. You may feel better.

Conclusion

With some effort, you can manage your mood. Medication can only get you so far. The rest—the living part—is up to you. To manage your mood well, you must live well. You must make decisions that better your situation. By trying these suggestions, you may feel better in managing your bipolar disorder. In fact, I believe, you will feel and do better. Make the effort to develop your life positively. It works for me and it will work for you.

Barbara Arner